East Devon Walks

Hugh Stoker

with sketch maps and photographs by the author

Mill House Publications
The Mill House, Seatown, Bridport, Dorset

CONTENTS

Introduction

EAST DEVON is criss-crossed by a captivating network of public footpaths, bridleways, cliff tracks, forest trails, prehistoric ridgeways, ancient drove roads and packhorse trials. To deal with them all in this pocket-sized booklet would be quite impossible, so instead I have concentrated on my own favourite walks in that wonderfully varied stretch of coast and countryside between the Exe valley and the Devon/Dorset border.

The walks follow a circular route, beginning and ending at a spot where the motorist can conveniently park his car without causing an obstruction. As for the walks themselves, their main objective is to seek out those beautiful and secluded places where you are most likely to see East Devon at its unspoilt best, and observe the wild creatures which live in it.

All the routes described are easily within the average walker's capabilities, but they *are* cross-country walks, and suitable footwear is therefore essential. The best choice for all seasons is a pair of sturdy waterproofed walking boots with non-slip cleated soles — worn, of course, with thick woollen socks. However, on the upland walks in dry summer weather you may prefer to wear cleated walking shoes. Smooth-soled shoes should be avoided at all costs; they are slippery on grass, and can be dangerous on steep hill slopes and cliff paths.

Although sketch maps have been included in this book, I would like to stress that a fairly large-scale Ordnance Survey map will add considerably to the enjoyment and interest of your walks. The best choice is undoubtedly the 1:25000 "Pathfinder" series, which shows all public rights-of-way and field boundaries.

An inexpensive pocket compass will also prove very useful when exploring some of the more remote and seldom-used routes. The coastal walks are obviously well-trodden, and the paths clearly defined. On many inland walks, however, there may be no visible path when crossing grassy fields and meadows — just the stiles and gateways linking various sections of a right-of-way. On these "off-the-beaten-track" sections I have purposely made my directions more explicit, and where necessary have included simple compass bearings for you to follow. You will find these bearings particularly useful when your next objective — be it stile, footbridge or gateway — happens to be hidden on the far side of a hill, or behind some overhanging tree branches.

Finally, do please observe the Country Code when sampling these walks. Don't park your car where it will obstruct a narrow lane, or prevent tractors and trailers manoeuvring into a field gateway. If you have a dog, keep it under control at all times. Keep it on a lead when walking in sheep country, or near woodland game reserves.

Enjoy yourselves!

Walk No. 1

Woodbury Castle and the Hawkerland Brakes

Woodbury Castle — Hawkerland Brakes — Hawkerland — Colaton Raleigh Common — Kettle Plantation — Woodbury Castle

Distance: Approx 6¼ miles

O.S. Map: SY 08/18 (1:25000); or 192 (1:50000)

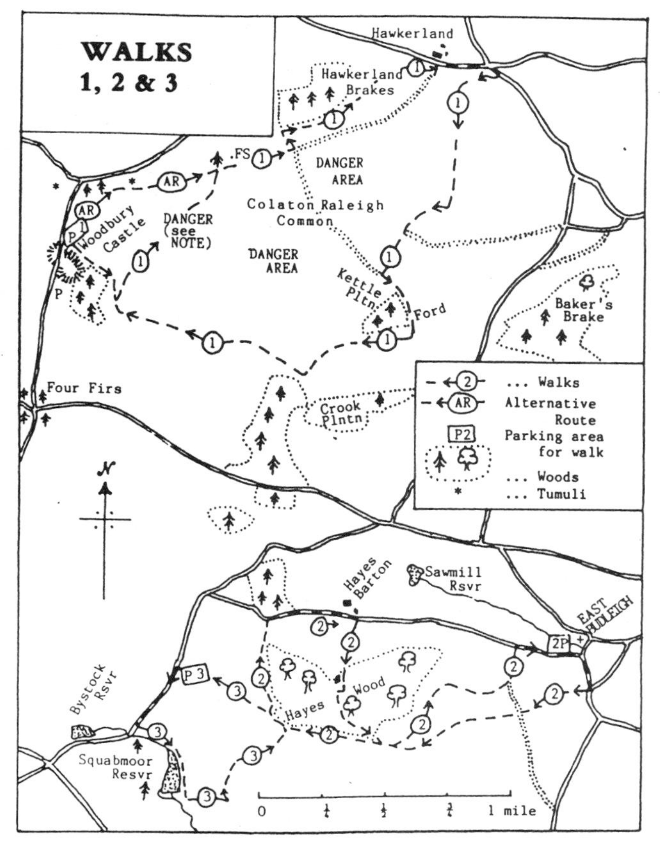

THE starting point for this walk is the free car parking area on the N side of Woodbury Castle. (See under *Points of Interest)*. Looking N from this car park you will notice a clump of pines dominating the skyline, with another similar clump to the NE. Your first job should be to check that no red flag is flying from a flagstaff alongside the NE clump. If it is, this indicates that the MOD firing range is in use. In this event I suggest you change your plans slightly, and sample Walk No 2 or 3 on nearby East Budleigh Common. (See NOTE).

However, assuming no red flag is flying, you set off from the parking area in a SE direction, following the track through the trees that skirts the earth ramparts of Woodbury Castle. Continue in the same direction beyond the hill-fort and alongside a large conifer wood. On reaching the SE corner of this wood you will see a track heading NE across a rolling stretch of common that in season is covered with flowering golden gorse and purple heather. Follow this track, and in due course it joins up with another track near the right-hand clump of pines that we mentioned earlier. Turn right along this track (it is classified as a public bridleway). After ¼-mile you will come to a place where the track is crossed by a footpath. This crossways used to be marked by a fingerpost, but at the time of writing all four arms are broken off, and only the upright post remains.

Turn left (NW) along the path which leads down to the SW corner of a conifer plantation called Hawkerland Brakes. Here you turn right (E), following a track which skirts the S edge of the wood. After a mile, and several changes of direction, the path brings you out onto a tarred lane near Hawkerland. Turn right (E) along this lane for ¼-mile, continuing straight on past a turning on your left until you come to a fork in the road. Take the right-hand fork; then after only a few yards turn right again on to a signposted bridleway. After a few hundred yards this track curves around to the S and follows the extreme edge of the common. At one point it passes close to a badger sett, and from the heaps of excavated earth one can see that its occupants have dug down below the stony top-soil of the heath into the rich red earth of Devon below.

Eventually, after curving around to the SW, the bridleway joins another ancient trackway at a primitive T-junction. Turn left (SE), passing an impressive stand of larches called Kettle Plantation on your right. Continue downhill until you come to a ford, where some stepping stones should enable you to cross the stream dryshod.

A few yards beyond the ford you bear right (W) along a rough but clearly defined bridleway across the heathery common. Continue along this track, which eventually bears around to the NW and brings you back to your parking place near Woodbury Castle.

NOTE: The public bridleway (marked "AR" on the sketch map) skirts the W edge of Colaton Raleigh Common — thus taking the entire walk outside the MOD range area. However, because there is always a risk that persons lacking local knowledge may stray unwittingly into the danger area, I still would not recommend this walk on days when the red flags are hoisted.

Points of Interest

Woodbury Castle. This ancient hill-fort has never been scientifically excavated, but it probably dates from the late Iron Age. Standing at a height of nearly 600 ft on the W edge of a vast tract of heathy common land, it is unusual in several respects. The massive ramparts, separated by a ditch over 20 ft deep, are overgrown with a beautiful grove of mature beech trees, amongst which flourish smaller clumps of rhododendrons and the occasional windswept pine.

A modern motor road, built on an ancient ridgeway, cuts through the W side of the hill-fort. Beside this road, and within the ramparts of the fort, a secluded cottage stands in a clearing among the beech trees.

During the Napoleonic Wars, because of its strategic position overlooking the Exe estuary, an encampment of British troops was stationed within this prehistoric stronghold from 1798 to 1803.

Walk No. 2

Raleigh's Birthplace

East Budleigh — Hayes Wood — East Budleigh Common — Hayes Barton — Hayes Wood — East Budleigh
Distance: Approx 5¼ miles
O.S. Map: SY 08/18 (1:25000); or 192 (1:50000)

THE starting point for this interesting walk is the free car park in Hayes Lane, just below East Budleigh church. This church contains many interesting features, and is well worth a visit. (See under *Points of Interest*).

From the church head S along High Street for about ¼-mile until, nearly opposite the school, you turn right (W) beside a farmhouse into unsurfaced Hayeswood Lane. Climbing steadily, this ancient trackway soon dwindles into a delightful green lane. Ignore all side tracks and keep heading between W and SW. Before long the lane skirts the S edge of Hayes Wood. Near the SW corner of this wood you continue up a gravelly track which leads you on to the edge of East Budleigh Common, but with the perimeter fence of Hayes Wood still close by on your right. On breasting a rise you'll see a disused brick rifle range butts on your right. Follow the track past this, and then continue roughly N, keeping just outside the W edge of Hayes Wood.

Eventually the track brings you to a gate which leads out on to a tarred by-lane. Turn right along this lane, which soon takes you past a beautiful old thatched farmhouse called Hayes Barton — famous for being the birthplace of Sir Walter Raleigh. (See under *Points of Interest*).

About 100 yards beyond Hayes Barton you turn right (S) along a signposted public footpath which leads you around the side of secluded Hayeswood Cottage. At the rear of the cottage the public footpath bears right and enters the shady depths of Hayes Wood. (NOTE: Dogs should be kept on a lead in these woods to avoid disturbing game). The path takes you through the centre of the wood, and then emerges through a gate at its S edge on to Hayeswood Lane.

Here you turn left down the lane for 150 yards before turning left again over a stile signposted: "Public Footpath". Follow this path across grassy fields in a NE direction, keeping a hedge close on your left all the way. After passing through one gate you will eventually come to another which leads you on to a farm track. This in turn leads on to an unsurfaced green lane. Turn left (N) along this lane, and soon you emerge on to tarred Hayes Lane. Turn right, and as you enter the outskirts of East Budleigh you'll pass a fine old cob and thatch house called "Vicar's Mead". Built in 1485, it was for centuries occupied by a long succession of local vicars. The last one to live in the house was Ambrose Stapleton, who held the living from 1794 to 1852. During those 58 years this forceful but well-loved man made his mark on all aspects of village life ... including the local smuggling trade which he personally organised with considerable success!

Points of Interest

East Budleigh and its Church. Some five hundred or more years ago, before the nearby River Otter silted up, this tranquil East Devon village was a thriving market town and seaport. Traces of this past association with the sea are to be found in the largely 15th century church of All Saints, where over 60 ancient carved bench-ends still survive. Some — including one of a North American Indian wearing a feathered head-dress — are believed to have been carved by returning sailors, possibly as a thanks offering for safe delivery from the perils of the deep. Another fine carving depicts an early 16th century sailing ship; whilst a pew on the N side of the nave, where the young Walter Raleigh used to sit with his parents as a boy, bears the Raleigh family arms and the date 1537.

Hayes Barton. Dating from the 15th century, and built of cob and thatch, the general appearance of this charming farmhouse remains very much as it must have been in Raleigh's day. The room in which he was born, about 1552, is situated in the west wing. One massive timber beam in the house is over 80 ft in length, and passes through five rooms. At the time of writing (1984) Hayes Barton is open in summer for coffee (Mondays - Saturdays) 10 - 12 am; and for cream teas 3 - 5.30 pm. Closed Sundays. For up-to-date information, however, you should consult one of the local Tourist Information Centres.

Walk No. 3

East Budleigh Common

Distance: Approx 2½ miles
O.S. Map: SY 08/18 (1:25000); or 192 (1:50000)

THIS short walk not only explores the beautiful furzy heathland of East Budleigh Common, but also descends into a delightful wooded coombe and takes you alongside a picturesque lake.

Your starting point is the large free car parking area situated approximately 2½ miles NE of Exmouth, alongside the unclassified by-road which runs from Exmouth up on to the common, passing Withycombe Barton and Bystock Reservoir on the way. After parking the car, return to the road and turn left (SW) downhill for ¼-mile until you come to a small pinewood near the bottom of the valley (NOTE: There is also limited parking space here among the trees). Turn left (SE) into this wood, still heading downhill until you join up with a track (classified as a public footpath) which leads you very pleasantly around the edge of tree-fringed Squabmoor Reservoir.

Immediately after passing the dam at the lower end of the lake, bear left (roughly E) up a steep gravelly track for about ⅓-mile until it joins another track. Here you double back sharply to your left and pass through a nearby gate. You should now be heading roughly N, with fenced fields on your right, and unfenced grassland on your left. Continue along this track until it takes you through another gate; then immediately afterwards turn right (E) on to a path through mixed woods and heathland which eventually brings you out on to a lane near the SW corner of Hayes Wood. Turn left here, and follow a track which heads NW across the common to your starting point.

Walk No. 4

Budleigh Salterton to Ladram Bay

Budleigh Salterton — Otterton — Ladram Bay — Budleigh Salterton

Distance: Approx 9 miles (full circuit); or 7½ miles (shorter version starting and ending near White Bridge — see NOTE)

O.S. Map: SY 08/18 (1:25000); or 192 (1:50000)

THIS walk explores a wide variety of coast and countryside, ranging from estuary saltings and lush riverside meadows to an old smugglers' lane and a cliff-top path that offers some magnificent views. For the amateur naturalist the walk is full of interest at any time

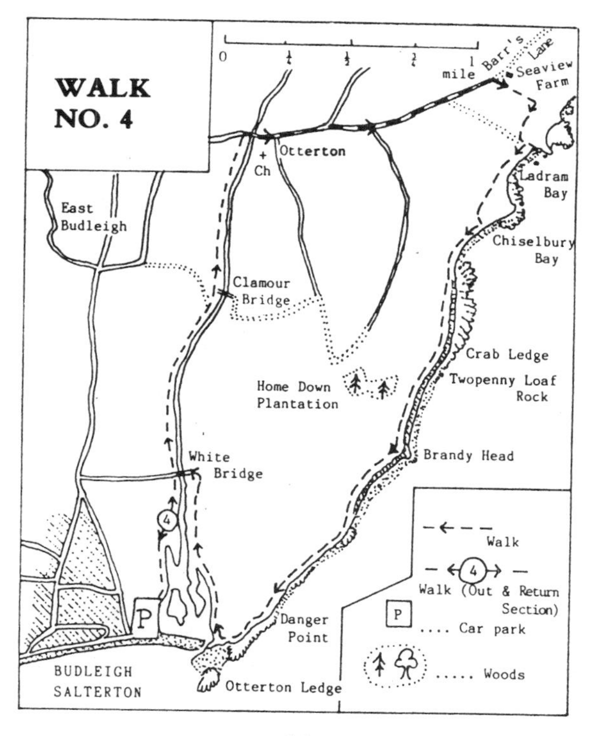

of year, but we particularly recommend you to sample it outside the holiday season, on one of those crisp, sunny days in winter or early spring. Incidentally, all the footpaths along this route are clearly defined, and remain firm and reasonably free from mud even in wet weather.

Motorists should park in the Lime Kiln Car Park, situated at the E end of Budleigh Salterton sea front. At the far NE corner of this car park you'll see a fingerpost indicating: "Footpath to Ladram Bay 3½ miles". Take this path, which runs close alongside the estuary of the River Otter — now classified as a Nature Reserve. Depending on the state of the tide, you are likely to see a wide variety of estuary birds, including waders, cormorants, herons, curlews and shellduck; whilst in severe winter weather the saltings may also be visited by flocks of wild geese — mostly Brent and Canada.

After about ¾-mile you come to the White Bridge. (See NOTE at end of the directions). DO NOT cross this bridge. Instead, continue N along the riverside path indicated by a fingerpost which reads: "Otterton 1½ miles".

By this time the river has become less tidal and swifter flowing. Beyond its far bank the hurrying waters of countless winter floods have worn away the lower slope of a steep grassy hillside, producing a low cliff of rich red sandstone. In many places this cliff is draped with dense curtains of trailing ivy, providing nesting cover in spring and summer for a wide variety of birds. Trees grow in jungle-like confusion between the foot of these cliffs and the river's edge, creating a strange contrast with the flat, meadowy western bank along which you are walking.

Soon you approach curiously-named Clamour Bridge. Here again you continue past the bridge, keeping to the W bank of the river. (DO NOT follow the waymarked path which curves away to the left, following the crest of a grassy embankment — this only leads to East Budleigh).

Eventually you come to the outskirts of Otterton. Here you turn right into the village across an old stone bridge. You may wish to pause awhile here to view the old manorial watermill, which has been restored and is now open to the public as a working museum. There is evidence to indicate that a mill has occupied this site since medieval times. (See also under *Points of Interest*).

About 1/3-mile up Otterton's main street you will see a narrow lane signposted: "Ladram Bay". Continue roughly E along this, and after a steady climb you'll come to a private caravan site road signposted: "Ladram Bay". Ignore this road and continue straight on (NE) for another 300 yards. This will bring you to Sea View Farm, where you turn right (SE) down a narrow, high-hedged lane. This is the original road to Ladram Bay, and was the route used by the local smuggling fraternity when transporting contraband inland from what used to be a very lonely and secluded beach.

Soon, after walking the final 100 yards through a miniature gorge, you arrive on Ladram's pebbly beach. Backed by red sandstone cliffs, and guarded by spectacular wave-washed rock stacks, it is arguably the most beautiful bay along this stretch of the Devon coast. It is a good place to rest awhile and eat your sandwiches. Alternatively, there's a pub nearby, "The Three Rocks" — but it closes down in winter.

To begin the return stage of your walk, first retrace your steps up the mini-gorge until, just before reaching a recently-built house, you see a fingerpost indicating the W-going section of the Coast Path. Take this path, which leads you across a grassy field towards the cliff-edge. Still climbing steadily, the cliff-path skirts the edge of Chislebury Bay, and then continues high above the waves breaking around Crab Ledge and picturesquely-named Twopenny Loaf Rock.

Eventually you come to an old wartime look-out post. Just beyond this vantage point you are rewarded with a magnificent view of the South Devon coastline, stretching from nearby Brandy Head, past Straight Point guarding the Exe estuary, as far as Start Point.

In the opposite direction there are the spectacular red cliffs of High Peak and Salcombe Hill; after which the cliffs contain progressively less red and more white as your gaze sweeps on past Weston Mouth towards the dazzling chalk buttresses of Beer Head. Far beyond, in the hazy distance, you may also see the magnificent sun-gilt crest of Golden Cap — highest point on the south coast.

The cliff path now begins to descend gently towards the mouth of the River Otter. Here you bear right (N) alongside a belt of wind-gnarled pines, through which you obtain an elevated view of the estuary and the wild fowl feeding on the saltings.

After about ¾-mile the path brings you back to the White Bridge. Cross this and return S along the riverside path to your parked car.

NOTE: There is space for limited grass verge parking beside the lane leading to the White Bridge. (See map). By starting and ending your walk here you reduce the distance covered by about 1½ miles.

Points of Interest

Otterton is a pleasant and spacious village. A small stream flows alongside the main street before curving away around the village green. Most of the older dwellings of cob, thatch and local red sandstone date from the 16th and 17th centuries, but a thousand years before that the Saxons established a settlement here.

The Domesday Book (compiled 1085-87) records that Otterton then had extensive saltworks and a Sunday market. In the following century, during the reign of William II, a priory was built on the steep little knoll where St Michael's Church stands today. The old stone mansion beside the church originally formed part of the priory, but was converted to its present use when the priory was dissolved in 1539.

Walk No. 5

Harpford Woods

Distance: Approx 2¾ miles
O.S. Map: SY 09/19 (1:25000); or 192 (1:50000)

THIS short walk through ancient woods of beech and oak, and along a half-forgotten packhorse lane, is really superb. (For a longer version, see Walk No. 6).

To reach the starting point by car, turn N off the A3052 on to the B3176 (signposted: "Tipton St. John"). After about ¾-mile you'll come to a place (marked "P" on the sketch map) where one can park among the trees on the E edge of Harpford Wood. Walk into the wood along the public footpath indicated by a roadside fingerpost. Almost immediately you'll be confronted by a fork in this path. Bear right here; then turn left at a second fork a little further on. The woodland path now leads downhill, passing through a tunnel beneath a long-disused railway line.

On the far side of the tunnel you join up with another path. Turn right (W) here and continue downhill through the trees until you emerge on to a narrow tarred lane (Knapps Lane) on the outskirts of Harpford. This little village, with its church and several dwellings of cob and thatch, lies about 200 yards down the lane. Turn left if you wish to visit it; otherwise turn right, following the lane uphill until it ends at a bridge which takes you across the dismantled railway. After crossing the bridge you turn E along an ancient green lane - so narrow that it was obviously used by pack ponies rather than any form of wheeled vehicles. When I travelled this way in early May the hedges bordering this lane were ablaze with wild flowers. There were also some clumps of stinging nettles, so ladies would be well-advised to wear trousers!

Climbing all the way, the old trail eventually brings you to a kissing gate through which you re-enter Harpford Woods. Turn left along a well-defined path until you come to the NE edge of the wood, with a glimpse of the B 3176 road just beyond. Turn right and follow a forestry track which runs just inside the edge of the wood. Very soon this will bring you back to your parked car.

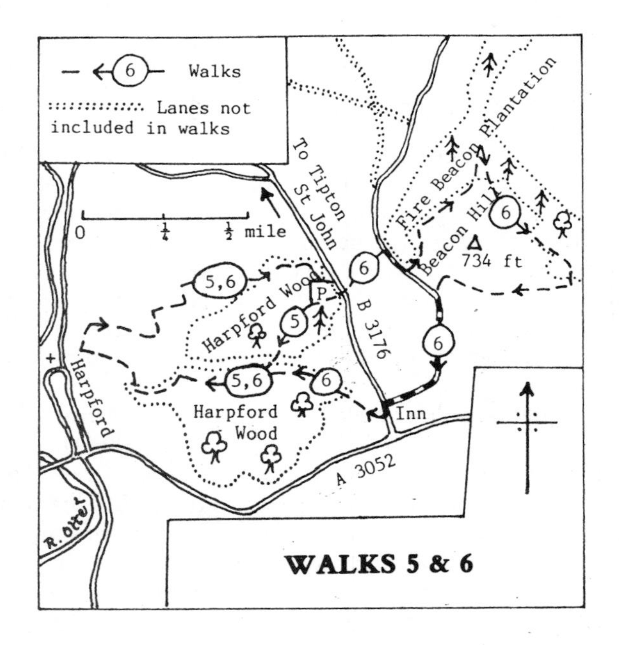

Walk No. 6

Beacon Hill and Harpford Woods

Harpford Wood layby — Fire Beacon Plantation — Beacon Hill — Bowd — Harpford Wood — Harpford village — Harpford Wood and layby
Distance: Approx 5 miles
O.S. Map: SY 09/19 (1:25000); or 192 (1:50000)

THIS walk is an extended version of Walk No. 5 and begins from the same car parking place marked "P" on the sketch map. Immediately opposite, on the other side of the road, you will see a gate with a fingerpost alongside it which reads: "Public Footpath to Fire Beacon" Follow this path uphill, keeping to the edge of the field to avoid damage to the crops. A stile takes you into the next grassy field - at the top of which some steps and another stile lead on to a narrow tarred lane. Turn right for about 100 yards; then left up a steep track which skirts the edge of Fire Beacon Plantation - a large stand of conifers.

Eventually the hilltop levels out on to a broad expanse of furzy common land, with grand views of the surrounding coast and countryside. After encircling the summit of Beacon Hill you rejoin the narrow tarred lane mentioned previously, and follow it downhill into Bowd. Here, if you have timed your walk sensibly, you can pause to refresh yourself at the Bowd Inn. Nearby, on the S side of the dismantled railway, a stile gives access to a public footpath which soon enters Harpford Woods. After about ¼-mile it joins up with the route previously described under Walk No. 5 and from here onwards you follow the directions for that walk until you return to your starting point.

Walk No. 7

Sidmouth to Ladram Bay

Sidmouth - High Peak — Ladram Bay — Sea View Farm — Barr's Lane — Sidmouth

Distance: Approx 4½ miles from Peak Hill car park; or 4¾ miles from Sidmouth sea front

O.S. Map: SY 08/18 (1:25000); or 192 (1:50000)

MOTORISTS are recommended to begin this walk at the large free car park at the top of Peak Hill, on the W outskirts of Sidmouth. Immediately opposite the car park entrance a gate leads on to a signposted public footpath which heads S across a grassy field towards the cliff-top. Here you turn right (W) and follow the clearly waymarked South Devon Coast Path. (See NOTE 1 if starting from Sidmouth sea front.)

After following this coast path for about ¾ mile you come to a three-armed fingerpost beside a large plantation of conifers. Follow the arm which reads: "Ladram Bay". This leads you through a kissing gate on to a broad path through the woods. (See Note 2). About 100 yards beyond the gate you'll see a narrower but well-used path branching off through the trees on your left. Follow this path if you wish to make a short diversion to the summit of High Peak. The summit is marked by an Ordnance Survey beacon standing in a small clearing among the trees, only a few feet from the cliff edge. It is a wonderful vantage point, providing magnificent views of the coastline as it curves away past Sidmouth and Beer Head towards the distance-hazed promontory of Portland Bill in Dorset.

From the top of High Peak another narrow path guides you downhill through the trees to rejoin the main path. Turn left (SSW) along this path, and very soon you emerge from the woods on to a pleasant cliff-top path. From here it is downhill all the way to Ladram Bay — noted for its spectacular red cliffs and wave-washed rock stacks. The bay makes an idyllic scene on a calm summer's day, but it can be an awe-inspiring place during a fierce onshore gale. An Italian barque was wrecked here many years ago during such a storm. In days gone by Ladram Bay was a very secluded spot, and for this reason the beach was frequently used by local smugglers when landing their illicit cargoes.

From Ladram you head inland up the *old* lane to Sea View Farm. Here you turn right (NE) along an old packhorse trail called Barr's Lane. After about ½-mile this leads you around the N perimeter of the High Peak woods before eventually bringing you back to the three-armed fingerpost that you passed on the outward stage of this walk. From here you retrace your steps along the cliffpath to your starting point.

NOTE 1: Non-motorists, starting on foot from Sidmouth sea front, need not follow the Peak Hill road all the way to its summit. Just a few yards beyond thatched Peak Hill Cottage you'll see a "Public Footpath" fingerpost on your left. Follow this path which leads you pleasantly upwards through a belt of trees, away from the road traffic. Soon, near the furzy cliff-top, you pass through a kissing gate and join the South Devon Coast Path.

NOTE: 2 The woods around High Peak are privately owned, and walkers using the public footpath should take great care against accidentally starting a fire. Also, please keep to the footpath, and if accompanied by a dog, keep it on a lead to avoid disturbing game.

NOTE 3: Readers wishing to extend this walk can conveniently combine it with Walk No. 8, which also begins and ends at the car park on top of Peak Hill.

Walk No. 8

Muttersmoor and Bulverton Hill

Peak Hill car park — Muttersmoor — Otterton Hill Plantation — Salters Cross — Bulverton Hill — Sidmouth Manor Woods — Muttersmoor — Peak Hill car park
Distance: Approx 5 miles
O.S. Map: SY 08/18 (1:25000); or 192 (1:50000)

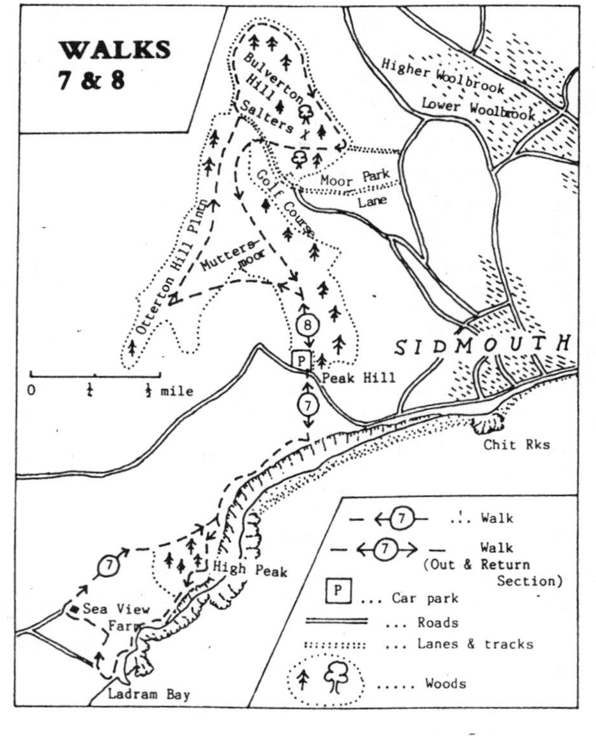

THIS walk starts at the large free car park at the top of Peak Hill about ¾ mile W of Sidmouth. At the NE corner of this car park you will see a fingerpost which reads: "Public Bridleway — Bulverton Hill 1¼ miles". Follow this track, which soon brings you out on to a wild expanse of furzy heathland, dotted with silver birch trees and wind-stunted pines.

Adjoining this heathland there are also numerous conifer plantations, and this mixture of open moorland and dense woodland provides a suitable habitat for a wide variety of wild life, including roe deer, badgers, foxes, stoats, grey squirrels and, of course, the ubiquitous rabbit. The species of birds are too numerous to list here, but in the woods around Bulverton Hill you are likely to see the brightly-plumaged jay, and the equally colourful green woodpecker.

About ½ mile after leaving the car park you will see a side-track, waymarked with a yellow arrow veering off to the left. Follow this track until it brings you to the edge of a large conifer wood called Otterton Hill Plantation. Turn right (roughly NE) and follow the wide bridleway-cum-firebreak which divides the edge of the wood from the neighbouring heath.

Continue along this track for about a mile until you come to a pair of fingerposts positioned close together at a place where four trackways intersect. This spot is known as Salters Cross, and it is said that the name dates back to medieval times when this ancient crossways lay upon the route used by pack ponies carrying salt from the extensive saltworks then sited along the local coast.

At Salters Cross you fork left downhill along a tree-flanked green lane that is signposted: "Back Lane". After about 200 yards you come to another fingerpost. Here you leave the lane and fork right (N) along a public footpath which curves around the flank of Bulverton Hill, keeping just inside the lower edge of an extensive larch plantation. This path has several twists and bends in it, and if you tread softly, and the wind is in the right quarter, you may surprise a few browsing roe deer. You will only catch a fleeting glimpse of them, however, before these wary creatures dash off into the depths of the forest.

The perimeter path curves around three sides of Bulverton Hill, providing pleasant views through the trees of the surrounding countryside. Eventually, after about 1¼ miles, it brings you to the SE corner of Sidmouth Manor Wood. Here, by a waymark post bearing yellow and blue arrows, you turn sharp right (WSW) along an attractive woodland bridleway (indicated by a blue arrow). Before long you begin to catch glimpses through the trees on your left of a narrow steep-sided valley called Bulverton Bottom. Shortly afterwards the track leads you out of the wood, and then curves SW across the head of the valley — which turns out to be the local golf course. On a sunny day the view down this valley is really superb.

Ignoring a left-hand fork which appears shortly after crossing the golf course, you continue SW along the bridleway until it joins up with another track. This intersection is marked with a three-armed fingerpost, and here you turn left along the track indicated by a "Peak Hill - ¾ mile" sign. This leads you directly back to your starting point in the car park.

* * * * *

NOTE 1: There is an alternative footpath route, commencing at Salters Cross, across the top of 680 ft high Bulverton Hill. This rejoins the described route on the NE side of the hill.

NOTE 2: Readers wishing to extend this walk can combine it with an ascent of High Peak. (For details, see Walk No. 7)

Points of Interest

Keble's Seat. Just a few yards N of Salters Cross is a green-painted seat, half-hidden among trees. According to local tradition it was here that John Keble, the famous English divine, wrote "Sun of my soul, thou saviour dear." Before the surrounding pine plantations grew up and blocked out the view, Keble's Seat provided a magnificent prospect of the Otter valley and the hills beyond.

Walk No. 9

Pen Hill and Hatway Hill

Sidbury Car Park — Pen Hill — Lower Knapp Farm — Lower Mincombe Farm — Mincombe Wood — Hatway Hill — Buckley Plantation — Buckley Dairy Farm — Sidbury
Distance: Approx 7¾ miles
O.S. Map: SY 09/19 (1:25000); or 193 (1:50000)

THIS walk treats you to a wonderful assortment of woodland, hill-top and lush valley scenery, and if possible you should sample it in spring when the wild flowers are in bloom.

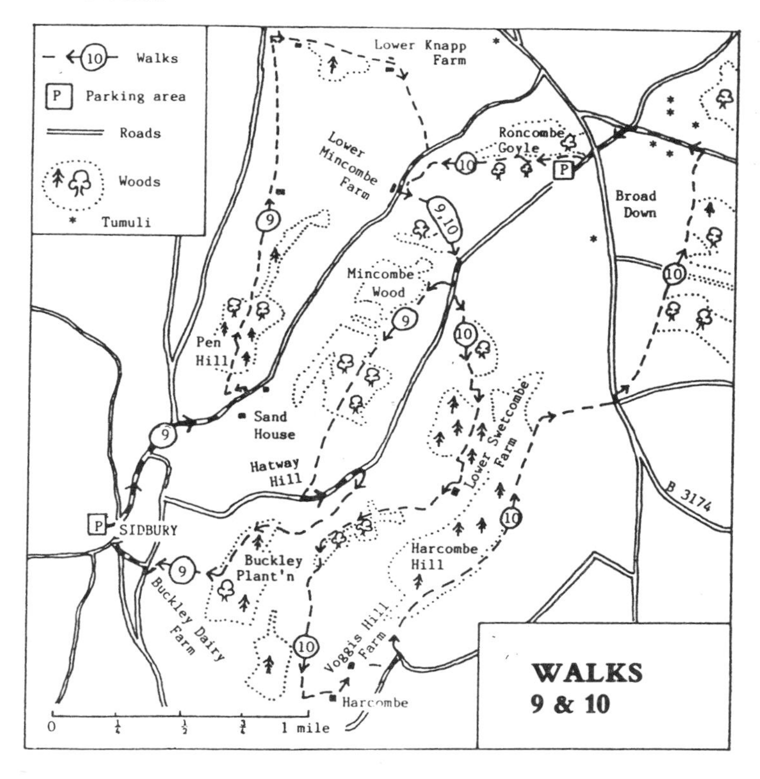

On leaving Sidbury's free car park, turn left (N) up the main street. Continue along this road (A375) for about ¾ mile until you come to a lane signposted "Roncombe", which forks off to the right. Head up this lane for ¼ mile, passing the entrance gates of the fine late-Tudor mansion called Sand Barton. (You will obtain a view of the house itself from the hilltops, later in this walk). About 100 yards further along the lane, turn left into a field gateway alongside a small corrugated iron barn.

Immediately after entering this field you turn left again, following the direction indicated by a "Public Footpath" fingerpost. After a few yards you'll come to the lower corner of the field — here you turn right and follow the hedge uphill towards a chalet situated picturesquely just below the wooded upper slopes of Pen Hill. On reaching the top left-hand corner of this field you cross a stile into the wood, and from here a path leads you through the trees to the top of Pen Hill. It's a stiff climb in places, but the magnificent view of the Sid valley and the distant sea will provide you with a good excuse to pause and regain your breath!

On reaching the crest of the hill, the path heads roughly N through a plantation of conifers. For most of the way it stays close to a boundary bank on your left, on which grow a line of much older deciduous trees. After about ½ mile the path crosses to the other side of this bank, and at the same time emerges from the wood on to an open expanse of grass, gorse and brambles.

Still keeping to the crest of the hill, you eventually pass a cluster of farm buildings and stock pens; then continue N along a rough -surfaced lane for ¾ mile until, by some more farm buildings, you turn right down a side track — classified as a public bridleway. After about 300 yards you leave the bridleway, bearing slightly right (ESE) through a gate, and follow a public footpath downhill a little to the left of a wood.

The path takes you down past Lower Knapp Farm, where you turn right along a concrete-surfaced access road that is classfied as a bridleway. This brings you on to a quiet tarred by-lane. Turn right along this lane for ¼ mile; then turn left at Lower Mincombe Farm on to a signposted public bridleway which skirts around some farm buildings and crosses the Roncombe Stream by a tiny stone bridge.

Climbing steeply, the bridleway takes you past the head of a small wooded goyle before emerging through a gate on to a tarred by-lane. Turn right along this lane for about 200 yards until you come to a fingerpost which reads: "Public Footpath to Sidbury". Turn right on to this path, which heads roughly SW across a grassy field, with Mincombe Wood on your right.

Soon, after leaving Mincombe Wood behind, you are treated to a grand view down the hillside into a deep combe filled with a patchwork of green fields and whitewashed cottages. Immediately ahead lies another wood, and the public footpath passes through it - still heading SSW. The wood is very wild and "jungly", and is the haunt of badgers, deer and foxes. In May it is carpeted with a misty haze of bluebells.

Eventually you emerge from the S end of the wood by climbing over a metal hurdle; then, immediately afterwards, you turn left through a gate and continue SSW across a grassy field, keeping a fence close on your right. This eventually brings you to a gate leading out on to a tarred by-lane.

Turn left uphill along this lane for about ¼ mile; then, near the top of the hill (Hatway Hill) turn right along a signposted public bridleway — a pleasant hedged green lane. After just over ¼ mile the lane makes a sharp left-hand bend, and at this spot you'll see a gate on your right leading into a narrow grassy field. A public footpath (not waymarked) runs WNW to the far end of this small field, where you pass through another gate into a beautiful mixed woodland known as Buckley Plantation. Follow the right-hand fork in the path, which leads downhill for a few yards before curving around in a SW direction just inside the lower edge of the wood. Continue in this direction until the path brings you to a stile leading out on to a grassy hillside overlooking Sidbury village.

Head straight downhill (slightly N of W) towards Buckley Dairy Farm, keeping a hedge on your right. On reaching the small grass paddock at the rear of the farmhouse you bear left towards a nearby dutch barn. Just beyond this barn the footpath emerges on to a tarred lane. Turn right along this lane; then left at nearby T—junction. This brings you back into Sidbury.

Walk No. 10

Roncombe Goyle

Roncombe Goyle — Lower Mincombe Farm — Lower Swetcombe Farm — Harcombe — Harcombe Hill — Rakeway Head — Bulhall Wood — Broad Down — Roncombe Goyle
Distance: Approx 8¾ miles
O.S. Map: SY 09/19 (1:25000); or 193 (1:50000)

THIS is one of my favourite wildtrack walks. The starting point at Roncombe Goyle can be approached by car along the B3174, which forks off from the A375 about 3 miles S of Honiton, and from the A3052 about 4½ miles W of Colyford. About 2-2½ miles beyond either of these turn-off points you will come to a minor crossroads. (DO NOT confuse it with the Y-junction known as Roncombe Gate, only 200 yards away). At this crossroads you turn SW down the lane leading to Barnes Surges and Sidbury. About 50 yards down this lane you'll see a "Public Footpath" fingerpost pointing off to the right. Park here on the wide grass verge and set off along the path, which takes you through a gate into a grassy field.

There is no visible track across the grass, so head WSW, aiming for a distant gap in the hedge. On your right the hillside falls away steeply towards a wood. The deep waterworn gorge known as Roncombe Goyle is hidden from view within this wood, and is the birthplace of the beautiful little Roncombe Stream which you will soon see flowing along the bottom of the valley.

Before long the footpath veers right (NW), heading downhill to a waymarked gateway among some trees at the bottom of the valleyside. Pass through this gate and immediately head very slightly S of W. Continue on this bearing until confronted by a hedge, where you turn right down a grass-grown track. Before long this track curves around to the left and brings you to an iron gate alongside a farmyard (Lower Mincombe Farm). Pass through this gate and turn left up a steeply rising track which is classified as a bridleway.

After passing through a narrow strip of woodland, the track veers S and eventually brings you to a gateway leading out on to a tarred by-lane. Turn right along this lane for about 200 yards; then turn left down a lane marked "Public Footpath to Harcombe". After passing a whitewashed cottage on your left the lane ends, and here you pass through a gate and continue along a grassy path which skirts the edge of a beautiful mixed woodland that is alive with birdsong in early spring.

Soon, on your left, you come to a gate which provides access on to another public footpath that heads off into the wood. Take this path, which wanders pleasantly downhill through the trees until it emerges through another gate into a small grassy field surrounded by more woods. Continue due S across this field to another gate and a narrow plank bridge over a ditch. (WARNING: This plank becomes very slippery when wet).

You now find yourself on a little-used cart track. Turn left along this for about 40-50 yards, then fork right off the main track on to a delightful woodland path which, although bordered by trees, is open enough to admit sunlight and provide magnificent views across the deep wooded slopes of Swetcombe — the "Sweet Coombe". This whole area is remote and rich in wild life, and if you walk quietly you may surprise a marauding fox or some browsing roe deer.

Eventually the path brings you to Lower Swetcombe Farmhouse, which you pass on your left while following a well-used tractor track (public bridleway). The track passes through a gate and heads SW across a grassy field. At the far side of this field the right-of-way bears right and skirts around the N (uphill) side of a long narrow wood which follows the contour of the hillside. At one point the path passes through a gap in an out-jutting spur of magnificent beech trees, but otherwise you remain just outside the perimeter of the wood. Dogs, of course, should be kept on a lead to prevent them from entering the wood and disturbing the wild life.

After a while the path takes you over a stile; then through a small gate. Immediately after passing through this gate you turn left (S) down a damp mossy hillside covered mainly with silver birch and bramble clumps. Ahead of you, on the far side of a hedge, you will soon see a grassy field. Bear right and follow this hedge until you come to a gate leading out of the wood. (WARNING: The ground near this gateway consists of deep, boggy peat, so approach it warily!)

After emerging from the gate, turn right (SW) along a little-used lane, which after a few initial twists and bends, heads almost due S along the side of a very picturesque valley, at the end of which lies the little village of Harcombe. On the outskirts of the village, beside the stream which flows down the valley bottom, you'll see a conspicuous thatched and whitewashed cottage. When you are almost abreast with this cottage you'll see a gateway on your left, and a public footpath (not waymarked) leading diagonally downhill across a field directly towards it. On reaching the cottage you follow the lane which runs beside it, using the small footbridge which spans the stream alongside a ford. Incidentally, when I passed this way I counted seven cats sunning themselves in the garden of this delightful cottage. Perhaps their numbers will have increased even more by the time you sample this walk!

A few yards further on you come to a tarred by-lane. Turn left along this, heading uphill past Voggis Hill Farm — where the lane degenerates into an unsurfaced track. This eventually brings you on to another tarred lane. Turn left along this until you come to a fingerpost which reads:

"Public Footpath to Blackberry Castle". (The correct spelling should be Blackbury). Follow this path, which gradually curves around to the right through pine plantations until it brings you to the top of Harcombe Hill.

Ignoring all side-paths, you continue along the main track in a generally NE-N direction. This takes you along the edge of an extensive area of woodland (Harcombe Hill Plantation) until, near the NE corner of the wood, you come to a spot where the track divides to left and right. Take the right-hand turning, which soon brings you to a tarred road. On the opposite side of the road, and some 30-40 yards to your left (at the far end of a small lay-by) you'll see a "Public Bridleway" fingerpost. Take this narrow track, which soon leads you into some very pleasant woods. At one spot the path passes close to the head of a wooded goyle, from the depths of which one can hear the sound of an underground stream emerging into the outer world.

Continue NNE along this track, which crosses a tarred private road leading to Wiscombe Grange — noted for its apple wines. About ½-mile further on the track leads you out on to a tarred road. Turn left along this, and then after 200 yards turn left again at a crossroads. After another 150 yards you will find yourself back at your parked car.

Points of Interest

Broad Down. The last mile of this walk takes you across Broad Down, which stands 768 feet above sea level. This greensand plateau extends NW to Farway Hill, and in prehistoric times a well-trodden ridgeway ran along its crest. This now lies beneath the present-day motor road. On either side of this ancient route are numerous tumuli (burial mounds), and historians regard this area as "the most important Middle Bronze Age necropolis in Devon outside Dartmoor".

Incidentally, in days gone by, the ancient crossways at Roncombe Gate, on the lonely heights of Broad Down, was used as a meeting place and "staging post" by smuggling gangs transporting contraband goods inland from Beer, Branscombe and Salcombe.

Roncombe Goyle. The word *goyle* (also *gwyle* in parts of neighbouring Dorset) is very ancient, but has survived in a few remote and hilly parts of the West Country where some Celtic words and traditions lingered on into medieval times. The word is used to describe a small steep-sided waterworn valley or ravine, usually thickly wooded.

Walk No. 11

By Cliffs, Forest and River

Salcombe Regis — Neroche Forest — Salcombe Hill Cliff — Sidmouth — Salcombe Hill — Neroche Forest — Salcombe Regis
Distance: 5½ miles
O.S. Map: SY 08/18 (1:25000); or 192 (1:50000)

THE sleepy little village of Salcombe Regis lies about 1 mile inland, hidden away in a deep fold in the East Devon hills, and the starting point for this walk is Salcombe's ancient church. (See under *Points of Interest*). There is a car park alongside the church for the use of visitors, and in return for this facility one can place a contribution towards the upkeep of the church in the collection box provided.

On leaving the church, head S down the lane which follows the bottom of the coombe. After about 500 yards turn right (SW) up a lane marked by a green-painted fingerpost which reads: "Footpath to Sidmouth".

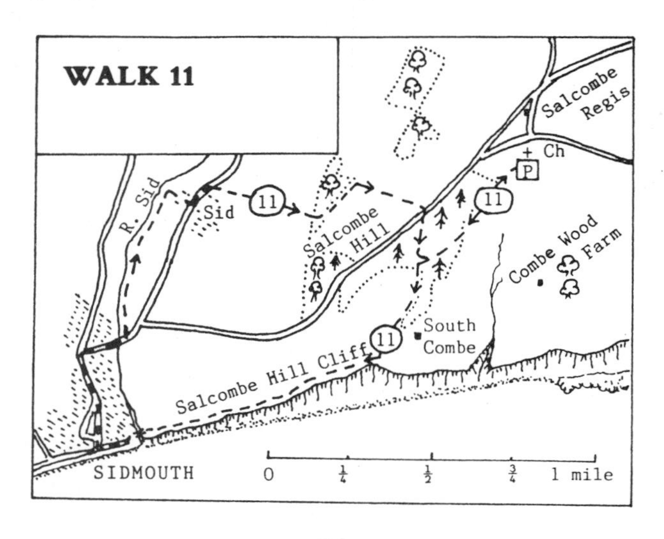

This lane skirts the edge of a dense wood that is part of the very fragmented Neroche Forest. After about ¼-mile you come to a fingerpost which reads: "Public Footpath to Sidmouth 1½ miles". Pass through a kissing gate on to this path, and follow it uphill through the trees until you come to another signpost where four paths intersect. One arm of this signpost points S and indicates a "link path leading to coast path". Follow this, and soon you'll arrive on Salcombe Hill Cliff, with the sea some 500 ft below. It is a lonely place of soaring gulls and wind-hovering kestrels. (See under *Points of Interest*).

Continuing W along the cliff path, you are soon treated to a gull's-eye view of Sidmouth and the beautiful coastline beyond. From this vantage point you descend towards the seaward end of Sidmouth by the cliff path. At the bottom you cross the mouth of the River Sid by a footbridge which was originally built in 1855 from timbers salvaged from a shipwreck.

After passing the cluster of winches and beached fishing boats, continue W along the sea front for about 200 yards; then turn right up Sidmouth's pleasant little main street. After ¼-mile you turn right into Salcombe Road. This soon brings you to the Old Toll House. Turn left here on to the footpath which runs alongside the river through a pleasant public park known as Sid Meadow.

After ½-mile you will come to a road heading off to the right. Follow this uphill until it joins the Salcombe road. Turn left for about 150 yards until you come to a fingerpost which reads: "Public Bridleway (Milltown Lane)". Turn right up this lane, which soon degenerates into an unsurfaced track. It is called Milltown Lane because, in days gone by, the farmers around Salcombe Regis used to bring their corn along it to a watermill situated on the banks of the River Sid. As you will soon discover, as you climb this steep and twisting lane, it was not a very convenient route!

Before long you come to a waymark post. Here you can take a short cut across the curve of a hairpin bend by continuing straight ahead (E) up a steep path bordered by woods. When I travelled this way I caught a brief glimpse of some roe deer disappearing through the trees.

On reaching the top of the hill your short-cut path meets up with the old green lane again. Turn left (NE) until after 300 yards the track curves around and heads ESE. At this point, if you glance across some furzy fields on your right, you'll see the telescope domes of the Norman Lockyer Observatory.

Soon the track brings you on to a tarred road. On the opposite side you'll see a stile and footpath leading into a pine forest. Head due S along this path, and before long it brings you back to the four-armed fingerpost which you passed on the outward stage of your walk. Turn left (ENE) down the path you previously climbed, and retrace your steps back to Salcombe Regis.

NOTE: You can, if you wish, just as conveniently begin and end this walk at (i) Sidmouth, or (ii) at the free car park situated on top of Salcombe Hill, immediately opposite the entrance to the Norman Lockyer Observatory. A link path connects this car park with the cliff-top path.

Points of Interest

Salcombe Regis Church contains several interesting features. They include: (i) *An eagle lectern* which dates from the 15th century. It is carved from a single block of wood. (ii) *The memorial tablet to Miriam Banister* who was born in Salcombe Regis parish on 19 March 1817, and died at St Louis, in the U.S.A., on 9 April 1928 at the age of 111 years! (iii) *The Lych Gate* leading into the churchyard. It is furnished with a large bolt made from the shaft of a giant "resurrection corkscrew" — an implement used by "body-snatchers" when hauling a partly-unearthed coffin from its grave. This one was abandoned when, in

Hayes Barton, near East Budleigh. This beautiful thatched farmhouse was the birthplace of Sir Walter Raleigh. (Walk 2).

Looking east towards Ladram Bay and High Peak from the cliff path leading to Budleigh Salterton. (Walk 4).

This view of the Harpford Woods footpath is framed by a tunnel beneath the disused branchline railway to Sidmouth. (Walks 5 and 6).

This charming cottage at Harcombe, with its neighbouring ford and footbridge, typifies the tranquil beauty of inland East Devon. (Walk 10).

Iigh Peak viewed from the cliff-top path above ;idmouth. (Walk 7).

Branscombe Church, looking south up the valleyside towards a wooded section of the South Devon Coast Path. (Walks 12 and 14).

Looking down on Beer beach from the coast path leading to Seaton Hole. (Walk 14).

Hooken Cliffs viewed from the path which leads down into the landslip wilderness of Under Hooken. (Walk 14).

the early 1800's, two Sidmouth doctors and a labourer were surprised in an attempt to steal the recently buried body of a Salcombe boy.

Salcombe Hill Cliff. Towards the end of the smuggling era, in the early 1800's, it was not unusual for cargoes of contraband to be landed on the beach below, and then hauled to the cliff-top on ropes. One night a preventive officer, with courageous devotion to duty, grabbed hold of a rope and allowed himself to be hauled up the cliff-face in place of the intended tub of brandy. The startled smugglers, on seeing his face appear over the cliff-edge, allowed the rope to slip from their hands, causing the unfortunate man to fall to his death.

Walk No. 12

High Cliffs and Deep Coombes

Branscombe Mouth car park or Branscombe Church — Weston Mouth — Slade House Farm — Salcombe Regis — Higher Dunscombe Cliff — Weston Mouth — Branscombe Mouth car park or Branscombe Church
Distances: Approx 11 miles from Branscombe Mouth; or 10 miles from Branscombe Church
O.S. Map: SY 08/18 (1:25000); or 192 (1:50000)

THIS superb walk explores some of East Devon's most spectacular coastal scenery, so if possible choose a fine day with good visibility.

In the itinerary at the top of this page I have shown two alternative starting points. During the peak holiday season, when car parking can be a problem in Branscombe village, you would be well advised to begin and end your walk at the car park immediately behind the beach at Branscombe Mouth. From here you head W along the coast path signposted: "Weston Mouth".

Outside the holiday season, from late autumn to early spring, it is often possible to find off the road parking space towards the W end of Branscombe village. You can then begin your walk by taking the signposted public footpath which picks its way among the tombstones on the S side of picturesque Branscombe Church.

Leaving the churchyard at its lower (S) end, you cross a plank bridge over a tiny stream; then continue S up a steep grassy hillside until the path enters a mixed woodland of beech, oak, ash, larch, pine and sycamore. Still climbing steeply, with several hairpin bends, the path leads you through the trees until it joins a broader track which runs E-W along the crest of the valleyside. This track forms part of the South Devon Coast Path, and here you turn right (W) and follow a series of fingerposts pointing the way to "Weston Mouth".

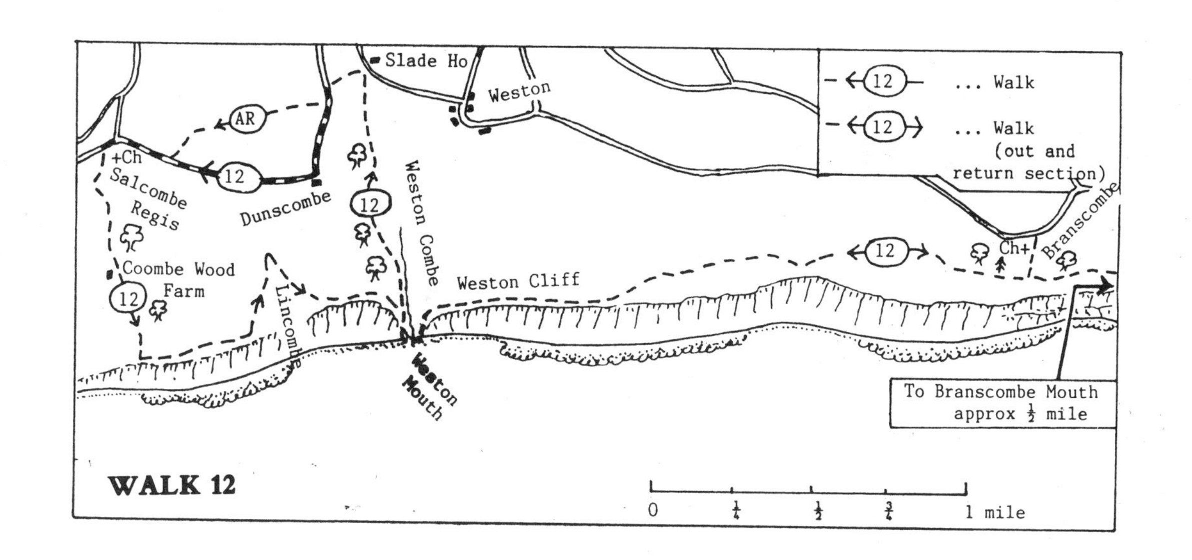
WALK 12
12 ... Walk
12 ... Walk (out and return section)
Slade Ho
Weston
AR
12
+Ch
Salcombe Regis
Dunscombe
12
Weston Combe
Coombe Wood Farm
12
Lincombe
Weston Cliff
Weston Mouth
12
Ch+
Branscombe
To Branscombe Mouth approx ½ mile
0
¼
½
¾
1 mile

Before long you leave the woods behind, and your route now crosses a succession of grassy fields before gradually drawing close to the tumbled weather-eroded slopes of Weston Cliff.

About ½-mile after joining the cliff path you arrive at a stile overlooking the steep, tree-flanked depths of Weston Coombe. Pause awhile by this stile to survey the next stage of your route. Immediately below lies Weston Mouth, where a tiny stream hurries through a miniature gorge (known locally as a "goyle"). Beyond the mouth of the goyle the stream loses itself among the pebbles of a lonely beach.

Cast your gaze to the far side of the coombe and you will see an area of woodland, marked on the O.S. map as Dunscombe Coppice. The second grassy field inland from the mouth of the coombe has this wood for its upper boundary, and if you look closely you will see a track climbing diagonally upwards alongside the edge of the trees before disappearing into the wood.

Your route lies along this track — but first of all, of course, you must descend from your present vantage point to the valley mouth. Here you cross the mouth of the stream by way of the beach. A winding flight of steps then leads you upwards to another grassy path signposted: "Dunscombe ¾M".

Head N along this path. Before long it curves around to the NW, and then enters the copse which you saw from your cliff-top vantage point.

Soon, on emerging from the upper edge of the copse, you veer right (N) off the main track to follow the fence bordering the wood. Although indistinct and not waymarked, this is a public footpath. In days gone by it was used by local smugglers when leading their strings of keg-laden ponies inland from the nearby beach. (See under *Points of Interest*).

The path climbs gently upwards through grassy fields, passing below a steep wooded hillside. In these woods the

1982 edition of the 1:25000 O.S. map still shows the site of a "Hermit's House". I have searched for the remains of this dwelling, but found only a large badger sett among the gnarled tree roots.

At the top end of the coombe the path leads you to Slade House Farm, where the pasture fields are enclosed by expensive ranch-style fencing instead of the customary barbed wire, and several of the outbuildings bear impressive notices, such as: "Isolation Ward", "Intensive Care Unit", etc.

This unusual farm is, in fact, the famous Donkey Sanctuary, which offers a life of ease and comfort to aged and unwanted mokes from all over Britain. It is the proud boast of this charitable institution that no deserving donkey is ever refused admission!

After passing through the Donkey Sanctuary the footpath brings you out on to a narrow tarred lane. Turn left (S) along this lane, which after about 1 mile brings you into Salcombe Regis. Alternatively, you could take a signposted right-of-way to the village across a succession of fields. ("AR" on map). I would warn you, however, that when I last walked that way the field path had been recently ploughed up, and the going was very muddy.

Salcombe Regis is a delightful little village, hidden away at the head of yet another deep coombe. It has an interesting church (see under *Points of Interest,* Walk No. 11); whilst over the door of the old thatched schoolhouse is carved the Biblical text: "Suffer little children...."

At the church you turn left (SSW) and follow the lane which runs downhill along the coombe bottom. After 300 yards you come to a gate, where a notice informs you that from here on the lane is a "Private Road to Coombe Wood Farm". However, it is also a public footpath, and you continue along the lane until, immediately beyond the farmhouse, a fingerpost indicates a side-path heading diagonally up the hillside to the left (SE).

This path, with one or two zig-zags, continues roughly SE and S until it brings you to the edge of Higher Dunscombe Cliffs. Pause here to admire the magnificent view of the South Devon coast, which extends as far as Brixham some 23 miles away. Beyond Brixham the distance-purpled cliffs of Berry Head and Scabbacombe Head conceal the estuary of the River Dart.

The coast path now leads you back to Weston Mouth, with a short diversion inland to skirt around the head of a beautiful little uninhabited valley called Lincombe. As you approach Lincombe you will pass a derelict lime kiln and numerous grassy hollows and mounds. In the 1700's lime burning was carried on here.

From Weston Mouth you retrace your steps along the coast path to your starting point at Branscombe.

Points of Interest

Slade House Farm. In smuggling days this conveniently sited farmhouse was just one of many places in the area where freshly landed contraband goods were hidden until such time as they could be transported safely further inland. There is a story of how, when Customs officers called unexpectedly at the farmhouse, the smugglers only just managed to destroy the evidence in time by emptying their tubs of brandy down a drain — from whence, shortly afterwards, there came the loud squeaking of inebriated rats!

Walk No. 13

Morganhayes Covert

Colyton — Heathayne — Ox Hill — Morganhayes Covert — Jobblehayes Lane — Sandpit Hill — Ridgway — Colyton
Distance: Approx 6 miles
O.S. Map: SY 29/39 (1:25000); or 193 (1:50000)

OF special interest to naturalists, this walk embraces a wide variety of scenery, ranging from lush riverside meadows to extensive hilltop woodlands. Although all the paths are easily negotiable, there are several unwaymarked sections which require the use of a compass.

Your starting point is the public car park in Colyton — a pleasant little town with ancient houses clustered

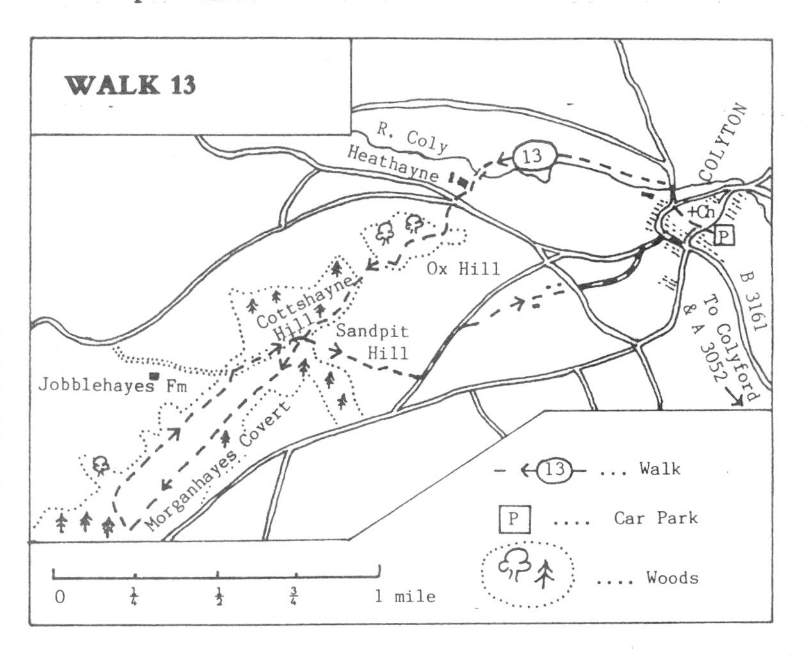

around a handsome church. Make your way first of all to the Bear Inn, which stands beside a picturesque stone bridge over the River Coly. Immediately after crossing this bridge you turn left along a riverside path. After following the river's meandering course for about ¾-mile you'll come to a footbridge. Use this to cross over to the S bank of the river, and then follow the path which leads uphill past an old thatched farmhouse called Heathayne. (See under *Points of Interest*).

Pass through the white-painted gate alongside the farmhouse on to a tarred by-lane. Continue uphill in a roughly S direction until you come to a spot where two other roads meet. A few yards W of this intersection, on the opposite side of the road, you'll see two gates positioned side by side in the hedge. Go through the right-hand metal gate, which is flanked by a "Public Footpath" fingerpost.

Just inside the gate you'll come to another fingerpost indicating the general direction of the path — a welcome aid because the path itself is often obscured by bracken. For the next few hundred yards you pick your way around scattered trees and bramble clumps, keeping as close as possible to the hedge of a grassy field on your right. Then, on reaching the S corner of this field, you steer roughly WSW into a wood of mature silver birch, larch, oak, ash and self-sown hollies. For the person without local knowledge a compass is almost essential here, because the undergrowth is criss-crossed by numerous badger and deer trails, and most of these are more clearly defined than the public footpath! (The badgers' sett is higher up the side of Ox Hill, near the S edge of the wood).

Your compass course will take you diagonally up the hillside, and should eventually bring you to a shallow "valley". Immediately after crossing this slight depression you'll notice faint traces of a long-disused cart track. Turn left (S) uphill along this old track, and very soon it will lead you to the remains of an old hunting gate set in the boundary of the wood. Do NOT pass through this gate; instead, turn right (W) along a clearly defined path just inside the edge of the wood.

About 150 yards along this path the perimeter fence veers around to the NW, and at this point the public footpath leaves the wood. At the time of writing a fallen ash tree has blocked the gap in the fence, but it is possible to scramble over the obstruction.

On leaving the wood you head SW across a grassy field, keeping a hedge close on your left hand. At the far side of this field you come to two gates. Pass through the left hand gate; then, immediately after, turn right across a stile leading into a conifer wood. Turn left (SSW) along a clearly defined path. At dusk and after dark this path is used by deer and badgers, and when the path is muddy you are likely to see their tracks.

Soon the path brings you to a spot where three lanes meet. One of them (Jobblehayes Lane) descends a steep hill on your right. Cross straight over this lane and continue in a roughly SW direction along a path leading into a dense forest of conifers. This path is usually churned up by horses, but one can avoid the worst patches by keeping to the edge.

If you consult your 1:25000 O.S. map you'll notice that this path is not marked as a public right of way. However, you may explore it with a clear conscience because these extensive hilltop woods are managed by the Forestry Commission, who take a friendly attitude towards walkers — provided they observe the Country Code. In particular, they ask you to take care against accidentally starting a fire. Also, if you are accompanied by a dog, it must be kept on a lead at all times.

Eventually the path brings you out on to a wide forestry road. Turn right and head downhill along this road for about ½-mile until you see a clearly defined footpath (not waymarked) doubling back into the trees in a slightly E of N direction. Turn right on to this path, which in places runs just inside the N perimeter of the wood, providing glimpses down into a deep meadowy valley backed by the distinctively shaped hill called Great Pen.

After about a mile this delightful path brings you out on to picturesque Jobblehayes Lane — an ancient track which makes its way up the wooded hillside from Jobblehayes Farm in the valley below. Turn right up this lane until you come to the crest of the hill visited earlier in this walk. Here you turn right (S) along a continuation of the lane for about 25 yards; then turn left (E) through a gateway into a grassy field and follow a gravelly cart track that heads downhill. As soon as you draw near to an old gravel pit you should bear right (ESE) away from the track, aiming for a gateway in the bottom right-hand corner of the field.

Pass through this gate and turn right along an unsurfaced lane until you reach a tarred road. Turn left down this road for ¼-mile until you see a stile and a "Footpath" sign leading off to the right from the grass verge. Cross this stile and head NE along a grassy footpath which runs alongside a deep tree-filled gulley. Before long the footpath joins up with a narrow lane, and from there on it is downhill all the way to Colyton.

Points of Interest

Heathayne. Although this ancient farmhouse has been repeatedly "patched-up" over the centuries with a mixture of stone and brickwork, it contains several interesting architectural features, including some of the original mullioned windows. A study of the O.S. map will reveal many other farms in this part of East Devon which have the suffix *hayne* or *hayes* in their name. This originates from the medieval English word *hay,* meaning "enclosure", and it is usually preceded by the personal name of whoever originally enclosed or farmed the land. (Local examples: Jobblehayes, Morganhayes, Weekhayne, Barritshayes, Andrewshayes, etc.).

Walk No. 14

Seaton Hole to Branscombe

Seaton Hole — Beer — Beer Head — Under Hooken — Branscombe Mouth — West Cliff — Branscombe Church and Village — Stockham's Hill — Beer — Seaton Hole

Distance: Approx 8 miles; or 6½ miles (shorter version starting and ending at Beer Head car park)

O.S. Map: SY 29/39 (1:25000); or 192 (1:50000)

THIS walk is a delight at any time of the year, but it is best done on a fine, clear day when the magnificent coastal and upland views can be enjoyed to their full advantage. Although the walk is described here as beginning and ending at Seaton Hole, about ½-mile W of the Seaton sea front, it can just as easily be commenced at Beer Head car park (opposite the Coastguard Station) or Branscombe Mouth car park.

From the seaward end of the small coombe at Seaton Hole you head up the narrow, high-banked lane that climbs the steep SW side of the valley. After about 200 yards you leave the lane and climb some steps in the left-hand bank. These lead you on to a pleasant footpath which follows the coastline around to the fishing village of Beer. From the vantage point of this cliff path you obtain a fine view of the cove, with its picturesque assortment of fishing craft drawn up on the shingle beach beneath the white chalk cliffs of Beer Head.

After descending into Beer village you head SW up the hilly road which runs alongside the allotments until you reach the Coastguard Station — easily recognised by its flagstaff. Here, opposite the Coastguard Station, you turn off along a narrow track called "Little Lane", which soon leads on to a grand stretch of the coastal footpath that takes you up over the grassy and furzy heights of Beer Head.

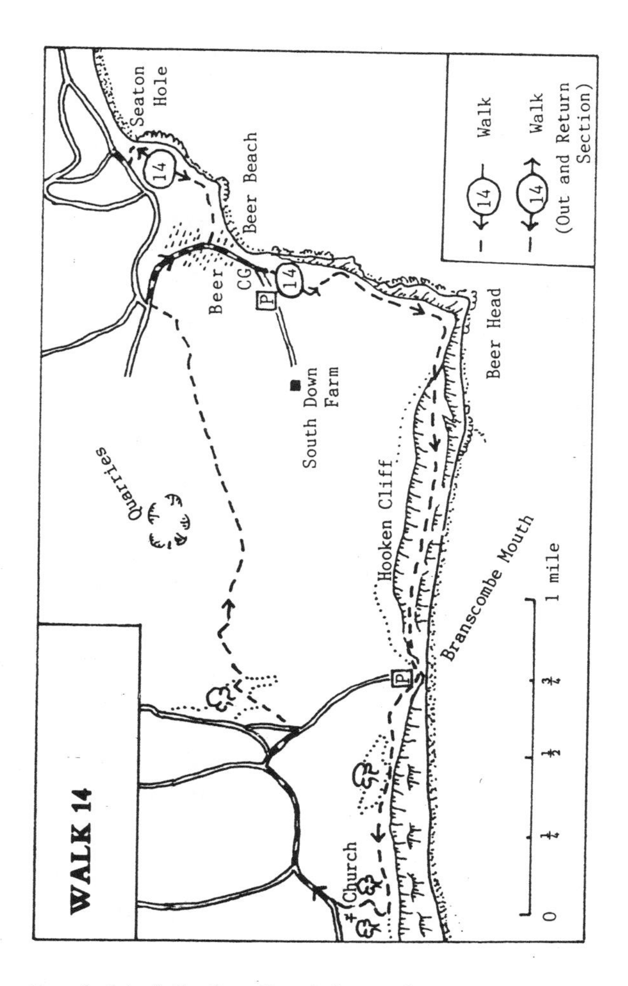

Just behind the headland the path curves around and heads NW towards the spectacular Hooken Cliffs, beneath which some massive landslips have formed a tumbled, jungly wilderness known as Under Hooken — the haunt of foxes, badgers and many other wild creatures.

Soon you come to a cliff-edge fingerpost indicating a choice of footpaths. Both have the same destination (Branscombe Mouth), but one path continues upwards along the cliff-top, whilst the other descends intriguingly into Under Hooken. Both routes are well worth exploring, but of the two I would recommend the Under Hooken trail as being more interesting, especially for the naturalist. Although bordered for most of the way by impenetrable thickets of blackthorn, elders and brambles, and by large craggy boulders covered with ivy, the path itself is easily negotiated. Far below, on your left, lies the sea and a sonorously murmuring shingle beach; on your right rises a lofty rampart of white, weather-eroded cliffs. At one point a side path leads up to an interesting-looking cave — doubtless once used by smugglers.

The undercliff trail eventually emerges from the wilderness into a scattered little community of cliff-hanging caravans. Back in the 1950's, while cruising down to Cornwall with a small sailing dinghy and a tent, I found this little cluster of wilderness-surrounded holiday hide-outs particularly intriguing when viewed from the sea. In those days, however, there were no caravans — just a random assortment of tar-coated chalets. They were more picturesque than today's aluminium boxes, although probably not so comfortable or convenient.

After descending into Branscombe Mouth you will find a footpath signpost immediately W of the tea rooms. Take the path leading to Weston Mouth, which climbs steeply up the grassy flank of West Cliff before eventually levelling out and providing some pleasant views inland of Branscombe village and its surrounding hills.

Before long you will see a footpath descending N towards the village — *ignore this,* and continue W along a track bordered by woods. After another ¼-mile you come to a second waymarked side-path, leading down towards the village. Take this path, which zig-zags down through a steep hanging wood of mixed larch, beech, oak and ash before crossing a tiny stream and leading you into Branscombe churchyard.

This beautiful old church, much of it dating from the 12th century, contains many things of outstanding beauty and interest, and should certainly be visited. (See under *Points of Interest*).

After leaving the church, turn right (NE) along the village street. Look out for the ancient blacksmith's forge on your left. Believed to have originated as a dwelling in Norman times, its recorded history goes back over 300 years. A notice by the smithy door tells us that around 1885 the forge was leased by the local Squire to one Fred Layzell, who passed it on to his son, Harry, who in turn retired in 1978, aged 82.

At the time of writing the building is still used part-time as a working smithy for shoeing and wrought ironwork, but it does possess one rather unusual feature — today the blacksmith is a lady!

After leaving the smithy, follow the curving road E and then NE for about ½-mile until, on coming to a fork, you turn right downhill past the "Mason's Arms" inn; then right again at the bottom of the hill. The lane now begins climbing again, and before long joins another very narrow lane marked with a "6 ft wide" warning sign.

Turn left (N) along this lane for just a few yards; then turn right (E) on to a National Trust waymarked footpath leading to Stockham's Hill. This takes you alongside a pleasant wood, and on the way passes two stiles which give access to a couple of woodland paths. Reluctantly ignoring these intriguing side-tracks, you continue uphill and before long enter an arable field, and then turn left keeping the hedge close on your left.

At the far end of this field you come to another stile bearing two waymark arrows, one pointing left to "Beer Quarry", and the other pointing roughly ESE across adjoining fields to "Mare's Lane, Beer". Follow the latter path, which soon leads you on to a pleasant green lane bordered by banked hedgerows.

After a mile or so the lane leads you alongside a miniature railway and down into the outskirts of Beer. Continue downhill, and then turn right towards the beach. From here you retrace your steps along the coast path to Seaton Hole.

Points of Interest

Branscombe Church nestles picturesquely beneath the wooded slopes of a tranquil, meadow-bottomed valley. Its squat fortress-like tower and adjoining parts of the nave were built around 1130, only a generation or two after the Norman Conquest. That an earlier church may once have stood on or near the site is indicated by the fact that masonry bearing typical Saxon herringbone chiselling is incorporated in the base of the tower's staircase turret.

Within the church is a Priest's Room — a most unusual feature dating from the days when the priest in charge actually lived in the church while attending to his numerous daily devotions. Notice the time-worn door and low "skullcracker" stone archway leading into the Priest's Room.

You should glance upward, too, and admire the ancient wagon roof above the 14th century chancel, with its original old oak beams.

On the north wall of the nave you will see an ancient wall painting protected by glass. Dating from about 1450, it shows a devil thrusting a spear through two figures (presumably male and female) dressed in red and blue. The picture is believed to represent a condemnation of Lust.

In the north transept you will find a fascinating memorial to Joan Wadham, who died in 1583, some five years before the Spanish Armada came sailing past this stretch of coast. Born Joan Tregarthin, this remarkable lady married twice — first to John Kellaway, of Cullompton, and later to John Wadham, of nearby Edge Barton.

Joan Wadham's memorial shows her two husbands kneeling face to face, whilst she is depicted kneeling meekly behind each of them, and accompanied by the children of each marriage. These would appear to number nineteen in all — fourteen (5 boys and 9 girls) fathered by John Kellaway; five (1 boy and 4 girls) by John Wadham. This last son, called Nicholas Wadham, was later to become famous as the founder of Wadham College, Oxford.

There are many other interesting things to be seen within and outside this charming old church, including a fine 14th century stone sedilia and piscina; an ancient stone coffin; a magnificent Tudor gallery with a carved oak front, and at the south-east corner of the chancel, a most unusual scratch sundial (possibly originating in the 14th century) on which the time-indicating shadow is cast by a nearby buttress. Due to its position, the sundial only shows the time until noon.

Walk No. 15

The Valley Where Time Has Stood Still

Musbury Church — Musbury Castle — Bulmoor Cross — Lower Farm — Combpyne Church — Musbury

Distance: Approx 6 miles (full circuit including visit to Combpyne village and church); or 4¾ miles (shortened version)

O.S. Map: SY 29/39 (1:25000); or 193 (1:50000)

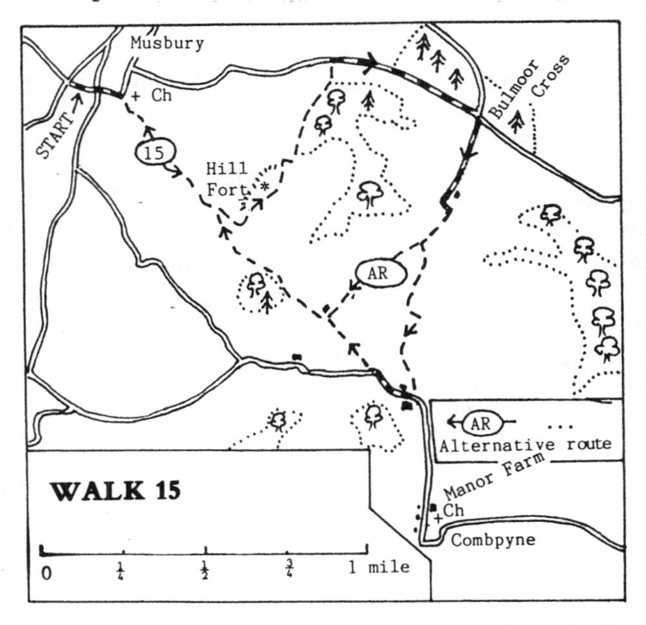

AFTER parking in Musbury (near the telephone kiosk is a good spot) head E up the village street to the church. (See under *Points of Interest*). Immediately alongside the church you take the waymarked private road (classified as a public footpath) to Musbury Farm. Pass the farm buildings on your left and continue uphill until, just beyond a sharp left-hand bend in the track, you come to a "Public Footpath" fingerpost pointing off to the right (SE). Follow this path across a grassy field and over a stile, and continue climbing uphill until you reach the summit of the Iron Age hill-fort known as Musbury Castle.

From the furzy, turf-covered summit of this vantage point you are rewarded with a magnificent view of the Axe valley and Beer Head. Turning your gaze southward, you also obtain a fine panoramic view of the deep and secluded Bruckland and Combpyne valleys, which you'll be exploring later in this walk.

You now continue roughly NE along the crest of the hill-fort, and then along the edge of an adjoining field, until the footpath brings you to a stile leading on to a narrow tarred lane. (See NOTE 1). Turn right (E) along this lane, which soon leads you very pleasantly alongside some extensive woodlands.

Eventually you come to a crossroads (Bulmoor Cross). Turn right (SSW) down the lane signposted: "Combpyne (Footpath only)". (See NOTE 2). After passing Bulmoor Farm and crossing a stream at the bottom of the valley, the surface of the lane suddenly deteriorates, and you find yourself walking along a rough and long-neglected medieval packhorse lane, which in places tunnels beneath over-arching branches of rampant hazels and blackthorns. It is rather like being transported back in time, and on rounding each bend in the track one half expects to encounter a string of heavily laden pack ponies bearing wares for Axminster market.

This time-worn trackway leads you steadily up the far side of the valley. Before long it joins another track, and here you turn right (SW). This soon brings you to Lower Farm, on the outskirts of Combpyne. From here the final return section of your walk lies down the lane to the right (W), but first of all I suggest you continue straight on for another ¼ mile or so into tiny Combpyne village — a delightful backwater of East Devon with a picturesque 13th century church. (See under *Points of Interest*).

After leaving the church, retrace your steps to Lower Farm and turn left (W) down the steepish hill. At the bottom of this hill the lane makes a sharp turn left, and here you'll see a "Public Footpath" fingerpost. Follow this path through an iron gate into a grassy field and head NW, keeping close to a hedge on your right. This brings you to a stile at the lower end of the field.

After crossing this first stile, keep the hedge facing you close on your right, and on rounding a bend in the hedge you'll come to another stile and a footbridge across a brook.

You now find yourself facing a house. The public footpath continues across a grassy field on the left-hand side of the garden hedge bordering the house. Head diagonally (NW) across this field, aiming for a gateway at the top left-hand corner. Pass through this gate and continue uphill, keeping a wood on your left.

Near the top corner of the wood you pass through a gap in a boundary bank, and then continue uphill in a NW direction. This brings you to a gate.

After passing through this gate, head slightly W of N until you come to a track. Bear right along this track, which leads you through a small wood of gnarled, moss-grown oaks. One venerable tree, visible from the path, is festooned with luxuriant clumps of ferns, which have found a roothold in natural "plant bowls" formed where the branches spring from the main trunk.

On emerging from the other side of the wood you find yourself under the flank of Musbury Castle, on the path you set out along on the opening stage of your walk. From here you retrace your steps to Musbury village.

NOTE 1: In places this lane is fringed by wide grass verges. Motorists could, therefore, use it as an alternative

starting and finishing point for this walk. This would reduce the length of the walk by approximately 1½ miles.
NOTE 2: (for walkers seeking a shorter route): On nearing the valley bottom this lane bends sharply left. A gate at this spot leads on to a public footpath which heads SW across a grassy field (keep close to the hedge); then, after crossing a footbridge, runs along the bank of a stream. It rejoins the route of the longer walk after about ½ mile. (See map).
The length of this shortened walk is approximately 4¾ miles if starting from Musbury village, or a mere 3¼ miles from the alternative starting point described under NOTE 1.

Points of Interest

The Church of St. Michael, Musbury, dates from the 13th Century, but since then it has been repeatedly enlarged and restored. The church stands in a very attractive setting, and contains the unusual Drake family monument. For 378 years, from 1415 to 1793, this family resided nearby in the ancient house of Ashe, traditional home of the local "lords of the Manor" since the days of the Norman Conquest. Unfortunately the old house was badly damaged by fire in 1644, and the present-day Ashe House was rebuilt some years later.

The memorial in the church, erected in 1611 and extended in 1646, shows three generations of Drakes kneeling in prayer. They include John Drake and his wife; their son Bernard and his wife, and Bernard's son, John, and his wife.

Bernard Drake made the sea his calling, and was knighted by Queen Elizabeth I for his success as an Admiral. In the end this very success was to prove his undoing because, after capturing a Portuguese vessel, he was obliged to attend the trial of prisoners taken with the ship. There, in the stuffy confines of the court room, he became infected with a fever. Realising he was seriously ill, Sir Bernard tried to return home to Musbury, but died on the way at Crediton, where his body was hurriedly buried lest it spread the infection. Certainly it must have been a particularly virulent fever, because as a result of that same ill-fated trial the judge, eleven jurymen and two other knights also died.

Incidentally, at the time of writing, there stands on top of the Drake memorial a facsimile copy from the Registers of Baptism of Musbury Church, recording that John, son of a Mr. Winston Churchill, was born on May 26, 1650. This John Churchill later became the first Duke of Marlborough, hero of Blenheim and other famous battles. His mother was Elizabeth, daughter of Sir John and Eleanor Drake.

The Church of St. Mary the Virgin, Combpyne, is mainly 13th Century. Situated alongside the ancient Manor farmhouse, the church possesses an unusual saddleback tower. A chalice and paten, nearly 500 years old, are still in regular use at the church. Another fascinating feature is the crude outline picture of a very ancient sailing ship on the S. wall. It was uncovered in 1950 during redecoration, and is thought to have been drawn by a 14th century sailor, perhaps as a thanks offering on his safe return to his native parish.

Walk No. 16

North of the Border

Tillworth Cross — Woodhouse Farm — Old Barn Farm — Pendragon — Southmoor Farm — Tillworth Cross
Distance: Approx 4½ miles
O.S. Map: SY 29/39 (1:25000); or 193 (1:50000)

THIS comparatively short walk explores a delightful but little known area of countryside just north of the border between Devon and Dorset. To reach your starting point at Tillworth Cross, take the B3165 road which branches off the A35 at Hunter's Lodge Inn, about 2 miles SE of Axminster. Some 2 miles along the B3165 from Hunter's Lodge (or 2½ miles from Marshwood if travelling in the opposite direction) you will see a narrow side-lane indicated by a signpost which reads: "Tillworth and Chard". Park the car on the layby just across the road from the signpost.

Set off down the side-lane. Soon you come to a cross-lanes. Head straight across (NW), and continue down a private farm road (classified as a bridleway). Soon you come to a gate bearing the sign: "Southmoor Farm". Do

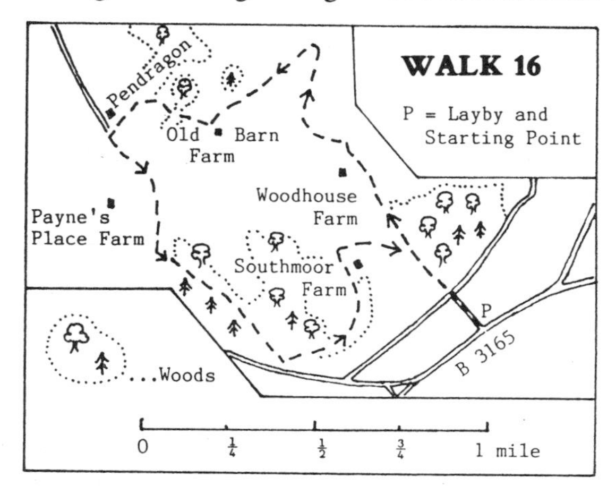

NOT go through this gate, but bear right and follow the lane until it curves sharp left and heads directly for Woodhouse Farm, visible only 100 yards away. At this point you continue NW down an unsurfaced green lane bordered by over-arching trees and bushes.

In winter the first few yards of this lane can be wet and muddy, but it soon improves and you can then enjoy a very pleasant downhill walk through mixed woodland. Soon the ancient track reaches the bottom of the valley and crosses a small stream. It now acquires a rather threadbare coating of tar, and begins to climb the opposite side of the valley. After ¼ mile you turn left into another green lane. It is marked by a "Public Bridleway" fingerpost, but being half-hidden by a rampant hedgerow it is easily missed.

After a few yards the bridleway bears left and, passing through a gate, brings you into a grassy field where all trace of the path disappears. Head SW, passing beneath a line of electricity pylons to the valley bottom. Here a small footbridge crosses a stream alongside a ford. (WARNING: The planks of this bridge become very slippery when wet).

After crossing the stream, continue SW up the opposite grassy slope. As soon as Old Barn Farm comes into view, aim a little to the right of the buildings. This will bring you on to the farm access track. Turn right (WNW) along this track, which soon begins to curve around through a mixture of rough pastures and scattered woodlands until it is heading SW.

Still climbing, you come eventually to a lonely house called "Pendragon", situated at the end of a tarred lane. At this point the bridleway you are following turns abruptly left (SSE) alongside a wood, before emerging into open pastureland.

Here you continue SE, keeping close to a hedge on your right. On coming to a gap in this hedge DO NOT follow the tractor track through it towards Payne's Place

Farm. Instead, continue alongside the hedge, which gradually curves around to the S.

Although you are still on the bridleway, there is little visible trace of it, so at this stage you must be careful with your map reading. DO NOT follow a grassy side-track which veers away from the bridleway in a SW direction, still following the line of the hedge. Instead, you must now part company with the hedge, and head diagonally across the field in a SE direction, aiming at a spot where the edge of a wood bordering the field makes a sharp right-angled bend.

On reaching the far corner of this field you pass through a gate and turn left (SE) along a clearly defined track, with woodlands on either side. Through the trees you catch glimpses of New Park House and the silvery glimmer of a lake.

Eventually you come to a fork in the track. Take the right-hand fork, and follow it uphill until it makes a sharp bend to the right. At this point you'll see a gate on your left giving access to tree-bordered bridleway. Follow this path, which sets off in an ENE direction, but then curves around to head NNW past Southmoor Farm.

Just beyond the farmhouse you join up with the farm access road (classified as a public footpath). This brings you back to the lane you travelled during the early stage of your walk. From here you retrace your steps to Tillworth Cross and the parked car.

Walk No. 17

Woodland Magic

St. Mary's Lane — St. Mary's Woods — Smoky Hole — Cathole Farm — Knoll Hill — Carsewell Farm — Yawl Hill — Yawl Cross — St. Mary's Lane
Distance: Approx 5 miles
O.S. Map: SY 29/39 (1:25000); or 193 (1:50000)

THIS highly recommended walk takes you through some very picturesque woodland scenery. It is a delight at any season of the year, although my favourite time is mid-May when the plantations of beech, ash and sycamore are ringing with birdsong, and the ground beneath the trees is carpeted with a hazy blue expanse of sun-dappled bluebells.

Your approach by car to the starting point of this walk lies along a narrow tarred byway called "St. Mary's Lane", which branches off from the A3070 approximately mid-way between Uplyme and the Hunters Lodge Inn. (This well-known pub is situated 2 miles SE of Axminster, on the A35). You will need to watch out carefully for the turning into St. Mary's Lane, because it is easily missed.

Drive along this lane for just under ½ mile until you come to a sharp hairpin bend. Just around this bend there is a small unsurfaced layby where you can park without causing an obstruction. DO NOT park on the passing places bordering this very narrow lane.

After parking the car you continue along the lane, which meanders through extensive mixed woodlands in a generally southerly direction. On your left a forested hillside falls away steeply, and through occasional gaps in the trees you catch glimpses of a lush and beautiful valley bottom, through which a small stream threads its way, linking a necklace of sun-glinting trout lakes.

For most of the time along this woodland stretch your only company will be the tree-muffled sounds of birdsong and the distant splashing of cascading water. Every now and then, however, the sylvan tranquillity is likely to be shattered by a shrill, echoing cry from one of the peacocks which lurk unseen in the valley below.

The lane takes you past the "Keepers's Cottage", and about ½ mile beyond this you come to a fork in the lane. Take the right-hand (uphill) fork. In just under ½ mile you will glimpse some dwellings bordering the lane a little way ahead, but before you reach them you will see a narrow lane forking off downhill to the left.

Follow this side-lane, and soon it will lead you past a secluded dwelling called "Smoky Hole". From here you continue along a rough waymarked footpath which curves around the wooded hillside in a generally SE direction before emerging on to another by-lane. A few yards along this lane you will see a "Public Footpath" fingerpost pointing off to the left. Follow this path, which soon takes you over a stile into a small grassy field.

Keeping the field hedge on your right, head roughly NNE and pass through a gateway near the far corner of the hedge; then turn left, still heading NNE, along the grassy valley of a small stream.

Soon, after passing Cathole Farm on your left, you come to a stile leading on to an intersection of three lanes. Turn SE up the right-hand lane. This soon leads you to the A3070 running through Yawl village. On the opposite side of the road you'll see two field gates. Pass through the right-hand gate and follow a public right of way into a grassy field. There is no visible path, but head uphill towards the top right-hand corner of the field where you will come to a stile in the hedge.

After crossing this stile you head roughly E., skirting the grassy slopes of Knoll Hill until you see Carsewell Farm buildings ahead. The right of way heads directly for the farm, where it joins up with a lane (classified as a bridleway) which runs between the buildings. Turn left

(N) along this bridleway until, after about ¾ mile, it joins up with a tarred lane.

Turn left (W) along this lane until, just *before* reaching a house called "Hunter's Moon", you come to a wayside sign which reads "Yawl Hill". A few yards to the right of this sign you'll see a small gate giving access to a public footpath. This runs W alongside the garden of a bungalow; then, emerging through another gate, it veers slightly N of W and continues alongside the left-hand hedge of a grassy field.

After following the right of way across two more fields, you eventually emerge through a gate on to the A3070. Turn right along this road for just a few yards; then turn left down a rough forest track which will soon lead you back to St. Mary's Lane and your parked car.

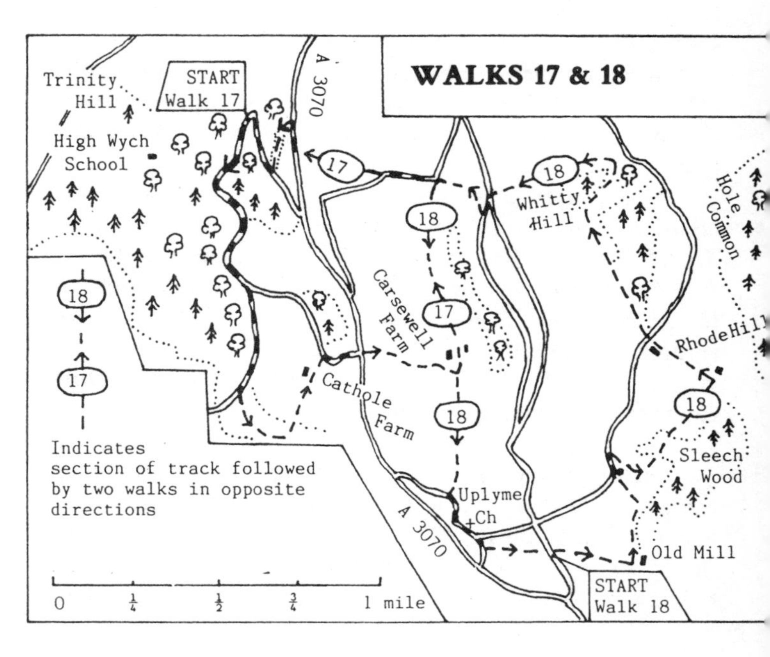

Walk No. 18

By an Old Mill to Whitty Hill

Uplyme (Mill Lane) — Old Mill — Rhode Hill — Whitty Hill — Carsewell Farm — Uplyme
Distance: Approx 5 miles
O.S. Map: SY 29/39 (1:25000); or 193 (1:50000)

TO reach the starting point for this very enjoyable walk, take the A3070 Uplyme - Lyme Regis road. About 100 yards NW of the Black Dog Inn take the side-lane signposted: "Rocombe and Harcombe". This lane winds downhill into the valley of the River Lim, and near the bottom of the hill it becomes wide enough in places to allow limited parking. (See also NOTE 1).

After parking the car, make your way to the old stone bridge across the Lim, and then turn E into Mill Lane. Before long this lane narrows into a tree-fringed bridlepath which picks its way precariously along the edge of a steep-sided goyle worn by the hurrying waters of the river.

Soon the path brings you out behind a picturesque old thatched watermill. Although still inhabited, it is sadly no longer a working mill. From here you turn left (N) along a concrete-surfaced bridleway which for the first ¼ mile runs alongside the edge of Sleech Wood and a small stream. This stream, incidentally, marks the boundary between Devon and Dorset.

Eventually the bridleway curves away from the wood and brings you out on to a tarred by-lane. Here you turn right uphill, passing after just a few yards a house called "Mulberry". Just beyond this house, by a small G.P.O. letterbox, you turn right down a narrow track (Hele Lane) which doubles back sharply to the SE; then curves around to the NE and dives into a wood.

On emerging from the far side of the wood you find yourself in open sloping pasture land, with a grand view of Hole Common Woods on the opposite side of the valley. (See NOTE 2). There is no visible path across the grass, but your right-of-way continues in a NE direction, following a line of electricity poles. After passing the third pole you will see a stile straight ahead. Cross this and continue alongside a paddock fence towards a nearby farmhouse until you come to another stile.

Cross this second stile; then immediately afterwards pass through a white kissing gate and turn left (W) up a tarred lane. After passing a large school house called Rhode Hill, you come to a T-junction. On the opposite side of the road, but a few yards to the left, you'll see a rough cart track bordered by a beech wood and a line of rampant holly trees.

Follow this uphill in a NNW direction. After ¼ mile, at a spot called Hodder's Corner, the main track turns sharply left, but your route lies straight ahead along a little-used grassy track. This soon leads you into a pasture field, where you continue NNW keeping close to the hedge on your left.

At the far end of this field you cross another stile. This brings you into a clump of scattered pines surrounded by open heathland. Continue straight ahead along a path leading towards a nearby pine plantation — pausing along the way to admire the magnificent views from this 600 ft. high vantage point.

When you arrive near the pine plantation you will see a path running through it, but as this is NOT a public right-of-way I cannot advise you to follow it. In any case, the other end of the path, where it emerges from the wood, has (at the time of writing) been blocked off with barbed wire. Your best plan, therefore, is to bear right and follow a narrow heather track which skirts around the perimeter of this small plantation. This will eventually bring you to the NW corner of the wood, where the right-of-way crosses into a grassy field.

This field is the summit of Whitty Hill (over 650 ft. high). Continue [illegible], aiming for the far right-hand corner of the field, where another stile brings you out on to a by-lane. Cross this lane and turn SSW down a fork in the lane for just a few yards until you come to a signposted footpath leading off to the right (NW).

This path leads you downhill past a small cottage to a grassy hollow below a farmhouse. Bear left (W) across this hollow to a nearby gate. After passing through this gate you will see a water trough just ahead. Turn right (NW) at the trough and pass through a nearby gate into another field. Keep the hedge on your left and soon you will come to another gate which brings you out on to a tarred lane.

Turn left (S) down this lane for just a few yards until it bends sharply to the right. Here you continue straight on (S) down an unsurfaced bridleway. For the next mile this track heads downhill, treating you to some intriguing bird's-eye views of the alternately grassy and woody slopes of Carsewell Bottom and Roccombe Bottom.

After passing between the buildings of Carsewell Farm the bridleway becomes a well-surfaced lane. On reaching the end of this lane, keep turning left until you come to Uplyme Church. Then, directly opposite the church, take the right-hand fork which leads down a short steep hill.

Near the bottom of this hill, alongside a cottage with the name "Brook Cottage" above its porch, you turn left (E) on to a footpath which leads you to the wooded banks of the River Lim — and then to the lane where you parked your car.

NOTE 1: Some readers may prefer to start and end this walk near the church at Uplyme. Roadside parking space can usually be found between the church and Lime Kiln Lane. Do NOT park outside the school next to the church during term time, as this causes congestion.

NOTE 2: Hole Common Woods are explored in *West Dorset Walks*.

Points of Interest

Whitty Hill. Situated some 2½ miles SE of Axminster, this hill probably owes its name to past associations with the Whitty family, who used to live in these parts. Indeed, the name is still encountered in East Devon. In 1755 one Thomas Whitty began manufacturing carpets in Axminster after being filled with admiration by the sight of some fine Turkish carpets in a London warehouse. After a good deal of trial and error he succeeded, with the help of his family and relatives, in weaving a type of carpet that was far superior to any hitherto produced in England. The business flourished, and before long Axminster carpets became famous throughout the world. Even the Sultan of Turkey ordered one in the early 1800's. He paid over £1,000 for it — a very considerable sum for those days.

Unfortunately Thomas Whitty's sons and grandson had less success with the business, and in 1835 the looms were sold and taken to Wilton, near Salisbury — which then became the home of "Wilton" carpets.

Since the end of the Second World War, however, a modern carpet industry has been developed in Axminster, and has helped to breathe fresh life into this small market town.

Walk No. 19

The Undercliff Nature Reserve

Distance: Optional (see text)
O.S. Map: SY 29/39 (1:25000); or 193 (1:50000)

THIS walk explores the unusual and very interesting stretch of coastline between Seaton, in East Devon, and Lyme Regis just across the border in Dorset. Although it has already been described in *West Dorset Walks*, I make no apologies for including it again in this booklet, because it really is rather special and should be regarded as a "must" by any keen rambler, naturalist or geologist visiting this part of East Devon.

The coastal cliffs between the mouth of the River Axe and Lyme Regis are very unstable, and subject to frequent landslips and rock falls. This is caused by underground water beneath the upper strata of permeable chalk and greensand flowing seawards over a sloping foundation of slippery impermeable clay. This constant trickle of underground water loosens the bottom layers of greensand, which then oozes slowly downhill, carrying its top-burden with it.

Occasionally — usually after a prolonged spell of wet weather — a landslip occurs of truly vast proportions. Perhaps the most memorable one took place at Christmas, 1839, when over half a mile of cliff-top land between Bindon and Dowlands slipped down overnight to open up a spectacular chasm hundreds of feet deep. In doing so it created an isolated plateau embracing some 15 acres of arable land, which was surrounded on all sides by precipitous chalk cliffs. This inaccessible "lost world" soon came to be known as Goat Island — although, of course, it was not an island in the true sense of the term.

Smaller and less spectacular landslips occur every year along this stretch of coast, and the overall length of the undercliff area is approximately 5 miles, and covers some 800 acres. Over the years a dense growth of trees and shrubs has sprung up, forming a sort of English "jungle" which is now the Axmouth - Lyme Regis National Nature Reserve. It is managed by the Nature Conservancy Council.

Badgers, foxes and roe deer are all present in the reserve, but being mainly nocturnal in their habits they are rarely seen. The diverse nature of the terrain, ranging from exposed cliff-face sun-traps to boggy woodland dells, results in a wide variety of plant and bird life. Some 400 different wild flowers (including some exotic garden "escapees" that have gone wild) and over 120 species of land and sea birds have been recorded here.

A section of the South Devon Coast Path runs through the length of the nature reserve. Although well maintained and clearly waymarked, the path becomes slippery and muddy in places during wet weather, so stout boots are advisable. Another point to bear in mind is that there are no intermediate escape routes from this "jungle path" to the outside world, so one must either complete the walk or retrace one's steps to the starting point.

To cover the entire distance from Seaton to Lyme Regis entails a walk of approximately 7 miles — 5 miles of which lies through the undercliff nature reserve itself, and the remainder along approach lanes and footpaths.

To make the outward and return journey therefore entails some 14 miles of fairly hard walking, which is probably more than the average rambler would wish to accomplish in one day. The best alternative, if it can be arranged, is to have someone give you a lift by car to Lyme Regis, and then walk back to Seaton or Axmouth. (Anyone based in Dorset would, of course, walk in the opposite direction). From both the practical and psychological points of view, this arrangement is far better than setting off on foot, and having a friend meet you with the car at the other end.

There is, unfortunately, no direct bus service between Seaton and Lyme Regis, although it is possible (Sundays excepted) to travel by bus between Seaton and Lyme Regis via Axminster. Be sure to check the timetable before deciding to do this, however, because most rural bus services nowadays are under constant threat of being curtailed or axed.

There are four main starting points for access to the Undercliff Nature Reserve, as follows:

From Seaton you cross the bridge over the River Axe; then a little further along the Axmouth road turn right up the lane leading to Axe Cliff Golf Club. (See NOTE below). From the club house the public right-of-way continues straight on across the golf links to a continuation of the lane on the far side. Soon you'll come to a fingerpost with four arms; turn right (SSE) here along a lane which ends at a gate leading into a grassy field. From here there is a waymarked field path leading to Bindon Cliff and the Landslip.

NOTE: Motorists can park on the layby beside the estuary road, near the golf club turn-off.

From Axmouth village you head uphill (SE) along Stepps Lane. After about ½ mile you'll see a stile and a "Public Footpath" fingerpost in the hedge on your right. Follow this path in a S direction across a grassy field until it brings you out on to a lane by the four-armed fingerpost mentioned in the previous paragraph. Then follow the waymarked footpath.

Stepps Lane. This quiet by-lane runs parallel with the coast between Axmouth village and Dowlands farm before joining the A3052 near Rousdon. At a point about ¼ mile E of Bindon Manor there is a small layby with limited parking space for a few cars. (IMPORTANT: Do not obstruct the field gate adjoining this layby). Immediately alongside this parking space you'll see an unsurfaced lane and a fingerpost which reads: "Public Bridleway (Link to

Coast Path)". Head down this lane, and soon you'll come to a four-armed fingerpost. Turn left and follow waymarked footpath.

From Lyme Regis. Motorists can conveniently set out from the large car park at the top of Cobb Road. From the lower SW corner of the car park a short cul-de-sac road leads on to a grassy hillside overlooking the sea. From here a field path wanders off in a W direction, leading you uphill to join a narrow by-lane which ends after about ¼ mile at Underhill Farm. At the end of this lane a footpath enters the nature reserve.

Points of Interest

Landslip Cottage. The first time I walked the undercliff path was as a small boy in 1932. Our objective on that occasion was the famous "Landslip Cottage", which in those days stood beside the path in a delightful tree-embowered garden. Here two elderly ladies used to serve teas to the hundreds of ramblers who travelled the path every summer.

An interesting story used to be told about "Landslip Cottage". Originally it had stood some distance back from the cliff-edge, but one morning many years previously its occupants had woken up to find that overnight a massive landslip had moved their home hundreds of feet, and it now stood upright and almost undamaged in a newly-formed bit of the undercliff "No-man's-land"!

That cottage is now a crumbling ruin, almost concealed by a mantle of ivy and the encroaching "jungle".